# Fields of Change

original story:
Jennifer Degenhardt

translator: Sofía Salazar

Cover and Interior Artist: Eli Delac

For Aaron and Alex. Thanks for the inspiration.

# INDEX

# ACKNOWLEDGEMENTS

Like so many of my stories, this one was inspired by conversations I had with my friend, Aaron, about how he grew up in Kansas in a place, time and manner so different from how I did. What struck me most about our chats was the focus on community and the people, staple themes for me in my stories. Certainly, this story does not tick off the culture boxes associated with Spanish-speaking regions, but it does inform about life in a small town and on a farm, and bits about agriculture in general. Believing what I do about awareness of how people live in places other than we do, this story was worth telling. Thank you, too, to Aaron's brother, Alex, for allowing me to use him as a character. After all, he IS the guy who works at a grain elevator, which inspired this whole story.

Thanks also go to the fine folks at the Wholly Cow Market for not only having a fun name, but for allowing me to use it in the story. It's a real place with real people who answer emails. Check it out at www.whollycowmarket.com.

The fabulous artwork was created by Eli Delac, a high school student at Centreville High School in Virginia. Eli is a student artist with whom collaborating is so easy. He is highly motivated, organized and seems to know exactly what is needed without too much direction. It is a dream to work with enterprising and ambitious young people. Thank you, Eli!

# Chapter 1
## Narrator

"Good morning, Trey," says his mother. "How are you today?"

Trey's mother is preparing breakfast for the family. In ten minutes, she has to leave for work.

"Good morning, Mom. I'm good. Excited," says Trey.

"Excited because it's the last day of eighth grade?" she asks.

"No, because summer football practice starts in nine days."

"Oh yeah, football..."

Trey's father enters the kitchen, yellow helmet in hand; the one he uses for work.

"Good morning, *familia*. How's everyone?" he asks.

"Dad, summer football practice starts in nine days," says Trey.

"Oh yeah? Great! Are you excited to play football in high school?"

"Yes, of course! I'm gonna be the best running back on the team. I want to run more than a hundred (100) yards a game – in every game."

"A hundred yards? That's a lot..."

Trey's mother sets down two plates with eggs, beans, salsa, and tortillas.

"Nona, *amor*, is there *chorizo*?" asks his father.

"*Sí*, Segundo. *Un momento*," she replies.

"Dad, I'm going to lift a lot of weights this summer. A lot... One hundred fifteen (115), one hundred thirty (130) …"

"Eat, Trey. You'll need to eat a lot more if you want to play football in high school."

Trey and his father, Segundo, eat their breakfast. His mother, Nona, leaves for work.

Twenty (20) minutes later, Trey's father grabs his yellow helmet and heads out, too.

*****

Segundo works at a grain elevator in Wichita, the largest city in Kansas. The grain elevator where he works is the biggest in the world.

Normally, Segundo works in the grain tower, but this morning the boss calls him into the office.

"Hello, Segundo," says Alex. "Thanks for coming."

"Of course, Alex. Is there a problem? Everything okay?" asks Segundo.

"Yes, please sit down," says Alex.

Segundo sits down.

"You know that the company plans to buy other, small grain elevators around the state," says Alex.

"Yes, I know. That's a great idea…"

"It's not public yet, but we're buying a small grain elevator in Johnson City," says Alex.

"Okay…"

"And our company needs a new boss for the new grain elevator there."

"Okay…"

"It's you, Segundo. You will be the boss of the new grain elevator," says Alex.

"Me? Why me?" asks Segundo. "I'm happy… but am I the right person for the job?"

"Segundo, you're the perfect person for the job," says Alex.

# Chapter 2
## Quinn

"Quinn," my mother says, "it's time."

It's 6:00 a.m. I have only a few minutes to get ready. I have to do my household chores before breakfast.

*Animals before people,* my mother always says.

*Animals before people,* I think.

In the kitchen, I greet my mother.

"Good morning, Mom."

"Good morning, Quinn."

There isn't much conversation. I need to take care of the animals.

We have a lot of animals: cattle, cows, sheep, and goats. We also have hens, pigs, ducks, horses, and, of course, cats and dogs. There are more animals than there are people!

We have:

-three (3) horses
-six (6) dogs
-seven (7) goats
-eight (8) cats: two (2) house cats and six (6) that live in the barn
-ten (10) cows
-twelve (12) ducks
-eighteen (18) pigs
-twenty-four (24) hens
-thirty-one (31) sheep

Where do I live? And why are there so many animals?

I live in Johnson City, Kansas. Johnson City is in the southwest part of Kansas. My family has had roots here for more than eighty (80) years. My family has a farm.

The farm has animals, and it also has crops. It's one thousand eight hundred (1,800) acres. In Stanton County, where Johnson City is, my family's farm isn't small, but it isn't big, either.

I arrive at the barn. My father is already there.

"Good morning, Dad."

"Hey, Quinn. The cattle need their food. And Sunday we're going to plant the second crop of corn. Will you help me?"

"Of course, Dad."

My father and I prepare food for all the animals. I like to see them in the mornings. They make me happy. I love living on the farm.

When we finish, it's 6:45 a.m. It's time for the people to eat.

"Dex and Quinn," says my mother, "here's your breakfast."

My mother has two plates with eggs and pancakes.

"Tressa, is there any bacon?" my father asks.

"Yes, Dex. One moment," says my mother.

"Here's some coffee."

"Thank you."

"Dad, football summer practice starts in seven days, in a week. I want to go. Is that okay?"

"Of course, Quinn. You're going to play football, right?"

"Yes, Dad. I'm very excited to play," I say.

"Playing football is amazing. Eat, Quinn. You have to eat a lot more to play football in high school."

My mother and I eat breakfast.

"Dex, are you going to get more information about the new company and your new position today?" asks my mother.

"Yes, I think so," says my father.

My father works on the farm, yes, but he also works at a grain elevator in Stanton County. He's the boss there.

He finishes breakfast and grabs his white helmet.

"See you later," my father says.

"See you later," my mother and I say.

My mother turns to me. "Quinn, are you ready? We have to leave in five (5) minutes."

Every morning, I go to school with my mother. She works at the same school where I'm a student.

# Chapter 3
## Trey

"That's it. Let's go," says my father.

My mother and I climb into the truck with him.

We're going to the new house in Johnson City.

"Bye, Wichita," says my mother. "It's time for a new experience!"

My mother is happy for my father. It's a new opportunity for him. He's going to be the new boss of the grain elevator in Johnson City.

I'm not as happy. I want to stay with my friends, go to high school with them, play football with them too. But now…

"Trey," says my father, "are you going to play football at school?"

"Yes…"

"Are you not excited?" asks my mother.

"Yes and no. I want to play football with my friends, but now…"

"Trey, tomorrow you and I are going to the school to find out when they start summer practices," says my father.

"The website says they start Monday, June 4 - in seven (7) days," I tell him.

"Okay, but we'll go to the school tomorrow to complete the forms," my father says.

"Mom and I already finished them," I say.

"Er... okay. Trey, this situation is hard for you, I know. But—"

"But it's a good opportunity for you and the family. I understand, Dad," I say.

"Why don't you look for more information about Johnson City?" asks my mother.

"Okay, Mom."

I take my phone, turn up the music, and start looking for information about my new city. Wichita isn't a huge city, but it's the biggest in Kansas; almost four hundred thousand (400,000) people.

I look up Johnson City on Google Maps. It's directly west of Wichita, in the southwest part of Kansas.

"Dad, where are we now?" I ask.

"We just passed Bucklin, and we're headed toward Montezuma."

I look up those towns online. Bucklin has a population of seven hundred nineteen (719), and Montezuma, nine hundred fifty-one (951). They're tiny.

Kansas is a rural state. We're deep in the rural part... Johnson City has to be bigger. It's a city, after all, right?

I type "Johnson City" in the search bar. Johnson City has a population of one thousand four hundred forty (1,440) people.

"Ugh," I say.

"What's wrong, Trey?" asks my mother.

"Mom, Johnson City isn't a city. It's small."

"It's going to be a new experience for all of us," says my father.

"Yes, a new experience," says my mother.

We're in the car for four hours. I see a lot, and I don't see anything.

What I do see:

• a lot of cattle
• a lot of sheep
• a lot of corn and other crops

- a lot of farms
- a lot of windmills

What I don't see:

- a lot of action

Ugh.

The experience is going to be new, but it isn't going to be better.

# Chapter 4
# Quinn

Immediately, I hear the alarm. It's 5:45...

"Argh!"

It's my father. He's in the barn.

I think: *Animals before people.*

I get up and put on my clothes to do my chores. At the door, I see my mother with the eggs for breakfast. She has eggs from the hens and from the ducks.

"Hi, Mom. Is there a problem?"

"Your dad is in a bad mood, Quinn. A few coyotes attacked the animals last night."

"Ah, but why is he yelling so loudly?"

"I don't know. Ask him."

I go to the barn and greet my father.

"Good morning, Dad."

"Not a good morning, Quinn," he says.

My father is very annoyed.

"What's the problem?" I ask.

"The coyotes attacked and killed three hens, two ducks, and a baby goat."

"That's horrible, Dad. But it's normal for us on the farm," I say to him. "Why are you angrier today?"

"We'll talk later. The cattle and the cows need their food."

"Of course, Dad."

My father and I prepare the food for all the animals. I like to see the animals in the mornings. Each animal has its own personality. They make me happy. I love living on the farm.

We finish at 6:45 in the morning. We enter the house to eat.

"Dex, drink your coffee," says my mother.

My father washes his hands and drinks his coffee. When he sits at the table, he sighs loudly.

"Ugh, the animals," says my father.

"Dad, it's normal on the farm. The coyotes come and attack the animals," I say.

"Quinn, your dad has other problems too," says my mother.

"Tressa, he doesn't have to know about that… You have to concentrate on football, Quinn."

"Dex, your son is fourteen years old. He has to

learn about the problems of life," says my mother.

"What's up, Dad?" I ask him.

My father takes another deep breath.

"Quinn, I didn't receive the promotion at my job," he says.

"I'm sorry, Dad. Do you know why?"

"The boss said the new company wanted one of their own. A man from Wichita got the position."

"That's bad news, Dad..." I say.

"But," says my mother, "we're happy. God blesses us. Your dad has a job."

"Yes, I have a job. And I need the job to keep the farm running," he says, sighing again.

My mother gives us our breakfast, and we eat in silence. Finally, she asks me about my plans for the day.

"Quinn, are you excited to start football practice this summer?"

"Yes, Mom. I'm happy to play football in high school..."

"...And that you don't have classes over the summer," my father says.

"Ha! You're right, Dad. But I also love working on the farm during the summer."

"Me too," says my father. "We need another worker. If a friend needs a job..."

"Okay, Dad. I'll ask."

As I clear the table, my mother speaks to me.

"Quinn, I'm going to wash the dishes. Get ready for your football practice. We're going to leave in fifteen minutes."

"Okay. Thank you for breakfast, Mom. And Dad, I'm sorry about the animals and your job."

"Thank you, son."

I go to my room. It's time to get ready for my first summer practice.

# Chapter 5
## Trey

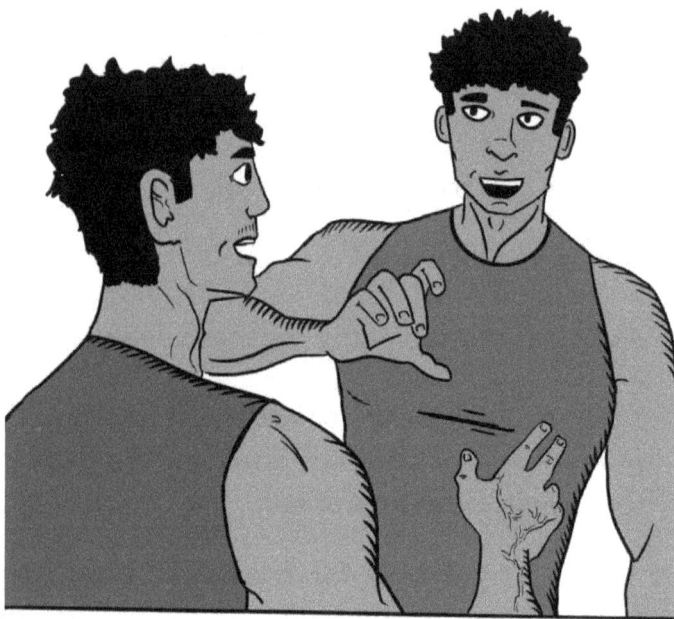

Finally, the day arrives. It's Monday, June 4th – the first day of summer football practice.

My father and I ride to school in his truck. We go to school first, and then he heads to his new job.

It's 6:45 in the morning.

"Trey, are you excited to start football?"

"Yes and no, Dad. Of course I love the sport..."

"That's obvious. How many yards do you want to run?"

"I want to run one hundred (100) yards every game, but..."

"But what? You don't think it's possible?"

"It's possible, but what if I don't play that position well? What if I'm not good? What happens if...?"

"Trey, you're just nervous. That's normal. You're going to run more than one hundred fifty (150) yards."

"Thanks, Dad."

We get to school after a six-minute drive.

"Here we are, Trey. Good luck. Have a great day."

"You too, Dad. Good luck at your new job."

*****

There's a group of more than twenty (20) boys near the football field.

"Hello," I say. "Are you guys here for football practice?"

An older, bigger guy answers, "Yeah. Are you new here?"

"Yes, my dad just got a new job here in Johnson City," I say.

The second boy looks more like me - younger and smaller.

"Welcome to Johnson City," says another boy.

"Thanks," I say.

"What's your name?"

"My name's Trey. What's yours?"

"I'm Quinn. Where are you from?"

"I'm from Wichita," I say.

"And where do you live now?" asks Quinn.

"We rented a house near the 4-H building. What about you?"

"Do you know where the municipal airport is on Route 160?"

"Yes! I know where the airport is."

"Do you know the farm Three Brothers?"

"Yes! There's a big red and yellow sign, right?"

"Yeah, that's my family's farm. I live there."

"The farms here are really big. How many acres?" I ask.

"Yes, they are big. Our farm is four hundred forty-five (445) acres. Aren't there farms in Wichita?" asks Quinn.

"Yeah, there are, but there are more here. Or they're bigger. Or… there's just more space," I say.

"Agriculture is important here in this part of the state," says Quinn.

"In Wichita too, but it isn't as obvious. Do you know Wichita, Quinn?"

"No, not really. I just know it's a very big city. How many people live there?"

"Almost four hundred thousand (400,000), I think," I say.

"A lot of people," says Quinn. "I prefer the countryside."

"I love the city. There's a lot to do – a lot of action."

"There's action here too," says Quinn. "Just a different kind."

"What do you do during the summer?" I ask.

"I work," says Quinn. "It's necessary. My family needs me to."

"Where do you work?" I ask.

"I work on the farm. Don't you have a job?" asks Quinn.

"No, I don't."

"Do you want to work on our farm?" Quinn asks.

At that moment, it's impossible to respond to his question. The coaches arrive at the football field and yell, "Okay, guys! Let's begin!"

# Chapter 6
## Quinn

It's Wednesday, 7:00 a.m., the first day Trey arrives at the farm to work with us. My father and I are in the barn.

"Hey, Trey. Welcome to our farm, Three Brothers. This is my dad, Dex Gerard. My uncles will come later."

"Hello, Mr. Gerard. Nice to meet you. Are you and your brothers the three brothers of the farm?"

"Hello, Trey. Very nice to meet you. Yes, we are three brothers – but we're not the original ones. They were my grandfather and his brothers."

"Wow. It's been your family's farm for a long time."

"Yes, it has. Are you ready to work, Trey?" my father asks.

"Yes, sir. I'm ready – but I don't know much about agriculture."

"Trey, that's not a problem. We'll give you a quick orientation," I say with a smile.

My father explains the work we need to do during the morning.

"See those irrigation pipes," he says.

Trey and I look at a pyramid of pipes. There

are more than a hundred (100) cylinders stacked up.

My father continues, "You guys need to put the pipes in the trenches we made yesterday with the tractor."

"Okay, Dad."

Trey looks from the pyramid of pipes to us again.

"Uh, um... do we do it by hand?"

My father and I glance at each other and laugh. It's clear that Trey is from the city.

"No, my friend. We're going to use the tractor. The pipes are sixteen (16) feet long with a diameter of ten (10) inches," I tell him.

"They're plastic, but they weigh a lot - about 4.2 pounds per foot," says my father.

"Yes, almost seventy (70) pounds each. They're heavy, so it's more efficient with the tractor," I say.

"Oh, okay," Trey replies.

My father gives us a few more instructions, then leaves for his job at the grain elevator.

"Let's go, Trey. Time for your agricultural training."

We climb onto the tractor and start to work.

After an hour of moving pipes under the hot sun, we stop to drink water and eat something. Trey asks, "With a farm of more than four hundred (400) acres, why don't you have more tractors?"

"We do. My uncle has the other one at his farm this morning. He'll bring it over later."

"He doesn't have his own tractor?"

"Not that kind. We share tractors because they cost a lot of money – it's more economical for our family."

I look at my friend. He's curious.

"Oh. How much does a tractor cost?" he asks.

"It depends. A used one costs around one hundred fifty thousand dollars ($150,000). A new one can be close to half a million dollars ($500,000)."

"Oh wow! That's a lot of money," says Trey.

"That's why it's more economical for our family to share them."

We work a few more hours and stop before lunch.

* * * * *

Finally, it's time for lunch. While Trey and I walk to the house, we overhear a conversation between my father and my uncle in the barn.

"And your job?" asks my uncle.

"It's horrible. The new director from Wichita is strict and demanding," says my father.

"But that's normal for a new boss, right?"

"Yes and no. It's different. It should have been my job, and now I don't know if I'll even have a position there in the future."

"Everything's going to be fine. Don't worry. Let's eat."

"Oh no," I whisper. "My dad needs that job. What's going to happen?"

# Chapter 7
## Trey

It's Sunday, the day of rest. After going to church, my parents and I go to a restaurant for lunch. Many people say that lunch at Wholly Cow is the best.

We talk about the last two months of our new life in Johnson City.

"Trey, how is football practice going?" my father asks.

I love the sport, and my father does too.

"It's good. We practice a lot and do a bunch of different exercises," I tell him.

"How many people are on the team?" asks my mother.

"There are like twenty-four or twenty-five in total. Not that many... that's why I have a chance to earn the running back position. I want to run a hundred yards..."

"We know, Trey," says my father with a smile.

At that moment, a server arrives at our table.

"Good morning. My name is Candy. Are you the family that's new to Johnson?"

My mother looks surprised but answers, "Yes. My name is Nona. This is my son, Trey, and this is my husband, Segundo. How did you know we were new?"

"As you can see, Johnson City isn't very big. News travels fast around here. My husband's brother works at the grain elevator. That's where you work, right?" asks Candy, looking at my father.

"Yes. I'm the new boss, from the Wichita company," says my father.

"I figured. News travels fast in Johnson. Ha, ha!"

Candy takes our order: three cheeseburgers, some French fries, and an order of macaroni and cheese.

"You have to eat well, Trey. You've got to be big and fast to play football."

"Dad, with all the exercises we do, and the work on the Gerard's farm, I'm going to have to eat a lot. Ha!"

"What do you do during practice?" asks my mother.

"We run, lift weights, and do other exercises. For example, one day we ran for twelve (12) minutes, did three sets of fifteen (15) squats, and lifted weights in the gym."

"And do you like working with Quinn's family?" my mother asks.

I think of those plastic tubes – sixteen (16) feet long, ten (10) inches in diameter, and weighing almost seventy (70) pounds each…

"Yes, I like working, but…"

"What's wrong, Trey?" asks my father.

"Yesterday when we passed by the barn, I heard a conversation between Quinn's dad and his uncle. His dad said that the new boss is strict and that he doesn't know if he'll keep his job for long. Was he talking about you, Dad? Are there problems at your new job?"

"There aren't problems at my job, Trey. There are always challenges when something's new," says my father.

"But why did Mr. Gerard say he might not have his job much longer?"

"Trey, don't worry about it. That's my problem, not yours."

"But Dad, Quinn is my friend…"

At that moment, Candy comes back to the table with the cheeseburgers, French fries, and mac and cheese.

"Great!" I say.

"Thank you, Candy," says my mother.

"You're welcome. And Nona, here's a list of useful information for living in Johnson City."

Candy hands my mother a list with local business names and directions to the nearest Walmart.

"Wow, thank you, Candy. How did you know...?" my mother asks.

"Ha! Everyone in Johnson City needs this list," says Candy, laughing.

"It's good to know the locals then," says my mother.

"Honey, if you don't know the locals, then you don't know anything," Candy replies with a smile.

We finish lunch and return to the rental house.

My father says, "Don't worry about it."

But I do worry.

Am I going to have problems because of my father's job?

# Chapter 8
## Quinn

It's July – almost August – and it's very hot outside. The sun is necessary for a farm, but the rain is too.

Stanton County is experiencing a severe drought. There's no rain. It's a problem for the farm and another problem for my father.

The coyotes came again and killed five (5) more chickens.

And my father still has problems at his job.

"Good morning, Dad," I say, walking into the barn.

"Hi, Quinn. I have another job for you and Trey today."

"Great, Dad. What is it?"

"As you know, we're in a drought. We're going to spread compost near the plants to help them retain more water."

"The compost helps?" I ask.

"Yes. The compost traps moisture and helps prevent erosion."

"I understand. Where are we going to start? Which part of the farm?"

While my father explains which field we'll start with, Trey arrives at the barn.

"Good morning, Mr. Gerard. Hi, Quinn."

"Hi, Trey," says my father. "Are you guys ready?"

"Yes, Dad. We're ready. See you later."

My father leaves without saying anything else.

He isn't happy.
He isn't happy about the coyotes.
He isn't happy about the drought.
He isn't happy about his job.

The last one is the biggest problem. My father needs the job at the grain elevator - but with the new boss, he doesn't know what will happen.

***** 

The heat is terrible; unbearable. We work hard spreading compost near the plants and stop every thirty (30) minutes to drink water.

During a break, Trey and I talk about the differences between Wichita and Johnson City.

"Quinn, how many people live here in Johnson City?" Trey asks.

"In Johnson City, I think there are about one thousand four hundred (1,400) people. In Stanton County, there are around two thousand (2,000)."

"You know a lot about this place. I'm impressed," Trey says.

"Trey, like you said – there isn't much action here. That's why we know everything that happens in town," I tell him with a smile.

"Quinn, it's a completely different life here. Did you know that the high school I was going to in Wichita has more people than all of Stanton County?" says Trey.

"No way! How many students go to that high school?" I ask.

"There are more than two thousand four hundred (2,400), but it's the biggest one in Wichita."

I take another sip of water and think for a second.

"Trey, how many high schools are there in Wichita?"

"I don't know. I'll look it up."

While Trey searches on Google, I look out over the fields. I love where I live. I love being on the farm. I'm not interested in city life.

"Here it says there are fourteen (14) high schools in the city of Wichita," says Trey.

"Wow! Fourteen high schools! Here we only have two schools in total: one middle school and one high school," I say.

"Ha, ha! I see that Johnson City is a little small. There are more churches than schools," says Trey.

"Churches are important here, Trey. They're the centers of the community. A lot of activities are organized by them," I tell my friend.

"It's incredible. This town is… so small."

I look at my new friend and think, *If Trey thinks this town is small, he's not going to believe the size of the high school.*

# Chapter 9
## Trey

It's August 15th, the first day of school. Today I ride to school with my father.

"Have a good day at school," my father says.

"Thanks, Dad. Have a good day at work," I tell him.

My father looks worried. There are problems at his new job.

"Thank you, Trey," he says quietly.

*****

It's lunchtime. All the students in seventh, eighth, and ninth grades eat together at the same time.

I see Quinn.

"Hey, Trey!" he calls. "How's your first day of school here in Johnson City?"

"Hi, Quinn. It's good; a little boring," I tell him.

"Trey, school *is* boring. It's…"

"It's not as boring in Wichita. There were a lot more people, more action, more activities," I say.

"Trey, you already know life is different here," says Quinn.

"Yeah, in Wichita the day goes by much faster."

"Time passes the same here," says Quinn.

"You didn't have a problem with time during the months we were working…"

"Of course not - we worked a lot, and time went by quickly. In Wichita..."

"Okay! In Wichita there are more people and more action. Johnson City isn't Wichita. Do you understand? You can't compare a town with a city - they're different," says Quinn.

"They're different, but the city is better," I say.

# Chapter 10
## Quinn

During lunch, Trey mentions Wichita so many times. *So many.*

*Wait!* I think at that moment. Trey arrived in Johnson City right when my father found out he didn't get the new position at work.

Trey's father has to be the new boss of the grain elevator!

"It's your dad!" I yell. "It's your dad!"

Trey looks at me, expressionless.

"It's *your* dad who's causing all the problems for my family!" I shout again.

Trey doesn't react, but all the other students turn to look at us, curious.

"I'm going to get you during football practice this afternoon. Be careful, *friend*. Be careful."

# Chapter 11
## Trey

School ends, and now it's time for football practice. I get myself and my equipment ready.

I think about the conversation that happened between Quinn and me earlier in the day: "It's your dad!" he yelled. "It's your dad!"

I looked at him, expressionless.

"It's *your* dad who's causing all the problems for my family!" he yelled again.

I didn't react, but the other students looked at us curiously.

After that, Quinn went to his next class, and we didn't talk about it again.

Now Quinn is getting ready for practice.

"Quinn," I say to him.

"Don't talk to me. Your dad took my dad's job. It's unforgivable."

"Quinn, I didn't know..." I say. "My dad didn't know either."

"You say you want to be the running back on the team? That position isn't going to be yours," says Quinn.

Again, I don't react. I don't know what to say.

\* \* \* \* \*

That afternoon's practice is brutal. The temperature is over ninety (90) degrees, and the humidity makes it worse.

It's also brutal because when Quinn plays defense, he tackles me on every single down. Once, I have the ball and I'm running toward the end zone when Quinn hits me hard.

"Dude," I say, "why are you tackling me so hard?"

"The position isn't going to be yours," Quinn snaps, still clearly angry.

Suddenly, we hear the sirens and horns of emergency vehicles echoing across Stanton County.

"It's not normal to hear that many at once," one boy says.

"They're going toward the grain elevator," says Quinn. "What's happening?"

"It must be a fire," says another. "The fire trucks only roll when there's a real emergency."

At that moment, the coaches shout, "Boys, we're done for today! We've been informed they need all available volunteer firefighters at the grain elevator. There's a big fire!"

Several players, who are also volunteer firefighters, sprint toward the school to gear up.

Quinn runs too.

"Trey, let's go! We need to get to the grain elevator. Something's really wrong."

We run together and climb into a truck with an older player.

Quinn looks anxious.

I don't know what's happening.

# Chapter 12
## Narrator

It's 5:30 in the evening. Segundo and Nona are with Dex and Tressa at the Wholly Cow restaurant to eat dinner before the game.

It's a Friday, two weeks after the fire at the grain elevator. It's also the first football game of the season. Trey and Quinn's team is playing against Elkhart.

Near the door, there's a newspaper with the headline:

*Fire at the Grain Elevator: Few Injuries Thanks to Quick Actions of Workers*

The article explains that there wasn't much damage to the structure or machinery thanks to the fast response of the workers.

The two couples sit at a table.

"Segundo, how's your arm?" asks Dex.

"It's better, thanks," says Segundo.

"That day was a perfect storm: the grain dust, the heat, and the men working on the machine. Lucky..." says Dex. "Lucky there wasn't an explosion."

"I was lucky, too," says Segundo.

"What do you mean?" asks Dex.

"I was lucky you knew where the fire extinguishers were and helped me get out."

"Of course, Segundo. That's what we do at work, we help each other."

"It's clear," says Segundo. "It's clear that

everyone helps one another. You're a good boss, Dex."

"You're a good boss, too, Segundo. I'm glad you're my boss," says Dex.

Nona looks at her husband and asks, "Segundo, are you going to tell him now?"

"Tell him what?" asks Tressa.

Segundo and Nona smile.

"Tell me what?" asks Dex. "Is it about work?"

Finally, Segundo looks at Dex and says, "I came to Johnson City to learn more about how the grain elevator operates. Before choosing a new boss, the company wanted more information."

Tressa and Dex glance at each other, nervous. They both know they need their jobs outside the farm to keep it running.

Segundo continues, "They told me, 'Segundo, evaluate the operation and determine what kind of person is needed to lead in the future.'"

"Okay… and?" says Dex.

"And I'm very happy to tell you..." says Segundo.

Tressa can't wait any longer. "Segundo, are you saying...?"

"I'm saying this grain elevator doesn't need a new person to do the job – because it already has one. It's you, Dex. It's you."

"Wow, Segundo. I don't know what to say," says Dex.

"You don't have to say anything. The position was always yours. The people in Wichita will be very happy with their new director of the grain elevator," says Segundo.

Tressa turns to Nona. "Will you have to return to Wichita immediately?"

Nona shakes her head. "No, not immediately. Trey needs to finish the school year first."

"Good. That means we have more time to enjoy each other," says Tressa.

"And if Trey wants a job next summer, he can work with us again," says Dex. "He's a hard worker."

\*\*\*\*\*

"Hey, Trey. Are you ready to play?" asks Quinn.

"Yes."

"But you would rather play your first football game with your friends from Wichita?"

"Yeah... how did you know?" asks Trey.

"You don't really mention Wichita anymore," says Quinn.

"I realized you were right. I used to talk about Wichita too much. But I don't live there, I live here now."

"You know the students from the film class always record the games and upload them to YouTube, right?" asks Quinn.

"No, I didn't know that. And...?"

"And, well, I know we're not in Wichita, but football is football. You can send your friends the link. We can all watch it together: your friends from Wichita and your friends here. What do you think?"

"Thanks, Quinn. That's a great idea," says Trey.

"But first, we have to win," says Quinn.

"Let's beat the Wildcats! Let's go Trojans!"

"Let's go Trojans!"

56

# ABOUT THE AUTHOR

Jennifer Degenhardt taught high school Spanish for over 20 years and now teaches at the college level. At the time she realized her own high school students, many of whom had learning challenges, acquired language best through stories, so she began to write ones that she thought would appeal to them. She has been writing ever since.

Other titles by Jen Degenhardt:

### BIBLIOSIMPLE
*Los chicos: Matías y Brayan* | The Boys: Matías and Brayan
*El viaje: José y Esmilda*

### LEVELED READERS
*Sancho en San Juan* | *Sancho in San Juan*
*Nuestro pueblo: San Juan la Laguna*
*La chica nueva* | *La Nouvelle Fille* | *The New Girl* | *Das Neue Mädchen* | *La nuova ragazza*
*La invitación* | *L'invitation* | *The Invitation* | *L'invito* | *Die Eindalung*
*Salida 8* | *Sortie no. 8* | *Exit 8*
*Salida 8 Questions & Practice*
*Raíces*
*Chuchotenango* | *La terre des chiens errants* | *La vita dei cani* | *Dogland*

*Con (un poco de) ayuda de mis amigos | With (a little) Help from My Friends | Un petit coup de main amical | Con (un po') d'aiuto dai miei amici*
*La última prueba | The Last Test*
*Los tres amigos | Three Friends | Drei Freunde | Les trois amis*
*La evolución musical*
*María María: un cuento de un huracán | María María: A Story of a Storm | Maria Maria: un histoire d'un orage*
*Debido a la tormenta | Because of the Storm*
*La lucha de la vida | The Fight of His Life*
*Secretos | Secrets (French) | Secrets Undisclosed (English)*
*Como vuela la pelota*
*Cambios | Changements | Changes*
*De la oscuridad a la luz | From Darkness into Light | Dal buio alla luce | De la obscurité à la lumière | Aus der Dunkelheit ins Licht*
*El pueblo | The Town | Le village*

 @puentes_language

 @Puentes Language Books
World Language Teaching Stories (Facebook group)

Visit www.puenteslanguage.com to sign up to receive information on new releases and other events.

Check out all titles as ebooks with audio on www.digilangua.co.

# ABOUT THE TRANSLATOR

Sofía Salazar is a bilingual high school student who lives in Connecticut. When she is not doing schoolwork, she plays soccer and participates in dance.

# ABOUT THE ILLUSTRATOR

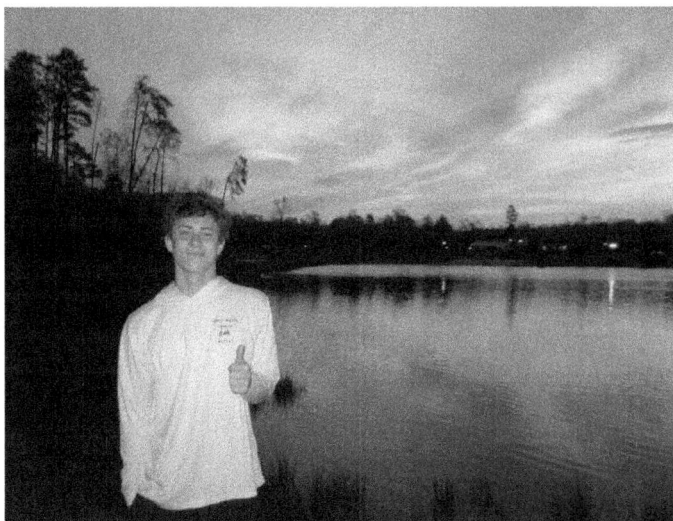

Eli Delac is a 16-year-old from Northern Virginia with a passion for illustration and art. Eli enjoys drawing, spending time with family and friends, and exercising. His passion for art drives him to pursue a career as a professional comic book artist after high school.

www.ingramcontent.com/pod-product-compliance
Lightning Source LLC
Chambersburg PA
CBHW060353050426
42449CB00011B/2963